CELEBRATING THE NAME TERESA

Celebrating the Name Teresa

Walter the Educator

Silent King Books

SILENT KING BOOKS

SKB

Copyright © 2024 by Walter the Educator

All rights reserved. No part of this book may be reproduced in any manner whatsoever without written permission except in the case of brief quotations embodied in critical articles and reviews.

First Printing, 2024

Disclaimer
This book is a literary work; the story is not about specific persons, locations, situations, and/or circumstances unless mentioned in a historical context. Any resemblance to real persons, locations, situations, and/or circumstances is coincidental. This book is for entertainment and informational purposes only. The author and publisher offer this information without warranties expressed or implied. No matter the grounds, neither the author nor the publisher will be accountable for any losses, injuries, or other damages caused by the reader's use of this book. The use of this book acknowledges an understanding and acceptance of this disclaimer.

dedicated to everyone with the first name of Teresa

TERESA

In the dawn's early blush, a whisper sings,

Teresa

A name as timeless as the moon's soft gleam,

Teresa

Teresa, where the heart's pure essence springs,

Teresa

In her name, a thousand dreams convene.

Teresa

Teresa, like a morning's first embrace,

Teresa

Her name, a melody of grace and fire,

Teresa

Each syllable, a step in life's sweet race,

Teresa

Her spirit, endless as the heart's desire.

Teresa

T for the tenderness in every smile,

Teresa

A beacon bright that guides through darkest night,

Teresa

R for resilience, steadfast through the miles,

Teresa

Her strength, a force that turns the wrong to right.

Teresa

E for the empathy within her soul,

Teresa

A gentle wave that soothes the fiercest storm,

Teresa

S for the sunshine making broken whole,

Teresa

Her warmth, a home where all are safe and warm.

Teresa

A for the artistry of all she dreams,

Teresa

A painter's touch upon life's canvas grand,

Teresa

Her visions, woven in life's golden seams,

Teresa

Each thread, a story from a gentle hand.

Teresa

Teresa, where the flowers bloom and grow,

Teresa

A garden lush with petals soft and bright,

Teresa

Her laughter, like a river's gentle flow,

Teresa

Her presence, like the dawn's returning light.

Teresa

In fields of green where wildflowers sway,

Teresa

Her name is whispered by the rustling leaves,

Teresa

The mountains echo back her name each day,

Teresa

A hymn of love that every heart receives.

Teresa

Teresa, muse to poets, artists, kings,

Teresa

A name that dances through the realms of time,

Teresa

Her essence like a bird on golden wings,

Teresa

Each moment spent with her, a gift, sublime.

Teresa

In moonlit nights where stars begin their waltz,

Teresa

Her name, a constellation in the sky,

Teresa

The constellations, envious, find their faults,

Teresa

For her light outshines even heaven's eye.

Teresa

Teresa, in the amber of the dusk,

Teresa

Her name, a lantern glowing in the mist,

Teresa

She turns the common into purest musk,

Teresa

Her touch, a blessing that none can resist.

Teresa

From ocean's depth to mountain's towering peak,

Teresa

Her name, a legend sung in every tongue,

Teresa

ABOUT THE CREATOR

Walter the Educator is one of the pseudonyms for Walter Anderson. Formally educated in Chemistry, Business, and Education, he is an educator, an author, a diverse entrepreneur, and he is the son of a disabled war veteran. "Walter the Educator" shares his time between educating and creating. He holds interests and owns several creative projects that entertain, enlighten, enhance, and educate, hoping to inspire and motivate you.

Follow, find new works, and stay up to date
with Walter the Educator™
at WaltertheEducator.com

www.ingramcontent.com/pod-product-compliance
Lightning Source LLC
LaVergne TN
LVHW012049070526
838201LV00082B/3880